Making The EXCEPTIONAL
NORMAL

Without Reengineering

Peregrine Press
St. Louis, MO

Peregrine Press
St. Louis, MO

Copyright © by Dale C. Furtwengler, 1997

Printed in the United States of America
November 1997

Library of Congress Catalog Card Number 97-97108
ISBN 0-9661478-0-4

This book is dedicated to
all who have or will
accept the mantle of leadership

Acknowledgments

We are only participants in what we accomplish. Those listed below are but a few who have lent their support and encouragement over the years. To each of them I extend a warm, heart-felt "thank you".

Charlotte, my wife, whose love supports me in more ways than I could ever have imagined. You are my life.

Cindy Boling, a dear friend and client, whose persistent requests for a reference manual provided the impetus for this book.

Charley and Jo Furtwengler, my parents, who taught my brothers and me care and concern for all whom we meet.

Mary Archer - St. Louis County Government, Andy Klemm - Klemm & Associates, Leslie Stambaugh - RLS Associates, Craig Stokely - The Stokely Partnership, Inc., Jean Stone of Interim HR Solutions and Kevin Wilcoxon - St. Louis County Government for their careful reading and valuable suggestions for the improvement of this effort.

Pat Martocci, Global Management Group, for granting permission to share her profound insight into effective communication.

There are countless others who have shared their kindness, generosity, knowledge and love. Some I remember vividly. The memory of others, those whose contribution I did not fully appreciate until later in life, has faded. The quality of my memory in no way diminishes their contribution or my gratitude to them.

TABLE OF CONTENTS

Introduction

Upon hearing the results achieved with the **Making The Exceptional** Normal system the listener asked, "And you accomplished that without reengineering?" Besides providing a subtitle, this gentleman reminded me of the plethora of improvements efforts employed in the last fifteen years, the limited success these efforts produced and the tolls they exacted upon the workforce.

The foundation for many of these improvement initiatives was laid in the 1960s when U.S. companies lead multinational growth. The competitive advantage enjoyed at that time caused managers of U.S. businesses to fall into the comfort trap. Profits were strong so managers didn't feel compelled to monitor spending. A manager's success was more likely to be measured by the size of the department than the results achieved. This combination of factors, complacency, strong profits and inappropriate success measures, not only invited competition, but created the need for radical surgery. Downsizing became the surgical tool of choice.

Radical surgery causes a lot of bleeding and tremendous amounts of pain. Downsizing was every bit as traumatic, but for many companies it was necessary for survival.

During the recovery period, managers realized that their companies had to stay fit to remain competitive. They could no longer take comfort in any advantage. Rather they needed to widen the gap between themselves and their competitors.

TQM (total quality management), benchmarking, activity-based costing, reengineering and other improvement initiatives were created to help companies improve their competitive standing. Each offers valuable approaches for improving results; yet, study after study shows that the CEOs of companies employing these tools are disappointed with the results. How can we explain the lack of results when the tools are conceptually sound?

I believe the answer lies in the implementation. In most improvement efforts the focus is on the desired result as it should be. Unfortunately, the focus often becomes so intense that the needs of the people, those responsible for producing the result, are overlooked. What impact does that have on the desired result? You can find the answer in your own experiences.

Remember a time when someone established new goals for you without considering your existing workload, the deadlines you faced or *your* goals. As your memory replays the event, allow yourself to experience the emotions that you felt at that time.

Think about how those emotions influenced your attitude toward those goals. Did you enthusiastically adopt them as your own or reluctantly comply with the directives?

How did your attitude affect your approach to the task? Did you do enough to protect your job or did you put all of your creativity, skills and experience to work for you?

The answers to these questions provide insights into the ways that your employees react when their needs are overlooked. If you don't consider their needs, they won't do more than comply with your requests.

My goal in writing this book is to share an approach to continuous improvement that balances goal orientation with the needs of the people who will make those goals a reality.

As you employ the techniques described in the **Making The Exceptional** Normal system, you will experience some very pleasant and unexpected surprises. Your employees will go beyond adopting your goals to helping you develop new goals. Together you will create a brighter future than any of you could have envisioned. Better yet, your staff will assure the achievement of those goals. Why? Because they participated in their creation.

The system outlined in this book is not a panacea. In fact, as my wife so insightfully noted, some managers will never adopt this approach. Managers who thrive on chaos, who don't feel complete or valuable unless they are fighting fires, aren't likely to employ this system.

Similarly, managers who possess a compelling need to be in control will not find this approach appealing. That's unfortunate. This system is designed to afford you, the manager, greater control, not as defined in the military command and control model, but through *influence*.

Conversely, managers who employ this system report that they and their team expend less energy while producing greater results. They also observe that both, they and their employees, share a renewed interest in their work Why? Because the work is more fulfilling which makes it more enjoyable.

Make your company more successful and, in the process, gain recognition for yourself and your team by **Making The Exceptional** Normal.

1

A Manager's Dream

In the blissful peace of slumber a manager dreams of:

- deadlines with reasonable time frames
- bosses who don't change their minds
- employees who know what they need to do, then do it well and on time
- everyone sharing the same vision and goals
- no communication problems
- everyone playing well together.

Ringgggg! Whew, that alarm went off just in time. You almost dreamed yourself out of a job. The reason the corporate world needs you is that you produce results in a reality that is 180° from the dream just described.

MAKING THE EXCEPTIONAL NORMAL

You live in a world of:

- half-life improvement efforts[1]
- customer demands that continuously change how your company does business
- employees striving for greater balance in their lives while the company requires greater productivity
- employees who don't enjoy their work
- conflicting goals
- miscommunication
- the ever present political battles and turf wars

It is your ability to make things happen despite all these obstacles that makes you valuable to your organization. The **Making The Exceptional** Normal system is designed to help you and your team become even more valuable to your company. An investment of less than two hours per week will enable your staff to *consistently* produce exceptional results. It is easier than you think and more fun than you can imagine.

---

[1] Half-life improvement efforts are breakthroughs that result in cutting the time for performing a task in half. For example, reducing the time for processing an order from two days to one day is a half-life improvement.

2

Exceptional Results

What constitutes "exceptional" results? A dear friend of mine, Pat Martocci, founder of Global Management Group, put into perspective the importance of using precise language. She said, "Each person who enters a discussion brings their own dictionary with them". In other words, no two people define a term in exactly the same way. Each person's definition is affected by their personal experiences.

This profound insight reminds me of the need to define "exceptional". Without a standard against which to measure new results how can we possibly determine whether these results are exceptional? Only by comparing current results against earlier performance can we make an appropriate judgment. Here are a few examples of results achieved with the *Making The Exceptional* Normal system, I'll let you judge whether they constitute exceptional results.

> **Mortgage Banking Operation** - I was hired as the assistant controller of a mortgage banking company. What I learned when I arrived astounded me. There were sixteen people in the department each working ten hours of overtime per week. At the end of fifteen working days they would abandon the computer system and manually prepare financial statements for the Board of Directors meeting.
>
> Within two months we (I did not do this alone) eliminated all overtime. By the end of the fourth month we were preparing financial statements on the computer. At the end of the first full year we had lost four degreed accountants. They were not replaced. With a 25% smaller staff and no overtime we closed the books at the end of the year in five working days with no audit adjustments AND we were developing new information to help other members of the management team become more effective.
>
> This staff produced more work in **16,000 fewer hours**. Half of those 16,000 hours were unnecessary overtime. The *Making*

The Exceptional Normal system produced a savings of 8,000 hours. What do you think? Would this meet your definition of exceptional results?

By the way, chapter 7 discusses how I eliminated the overtime without inviting a mutiny.

Construction Operation - Our search for a new computer system was completed just in time for a June delivery, the first of our four busiest months.

My staff and I agreed that we did not have time to maintain dual systems after conversion. Each of us committed to learn that portion of the software necessary to perform our normal daily tasks and to be a resource for the others on that portion of the software. Our conversion plan included the help of three temporary data entry personnel. Of course they needed supervision, so our plan included a reallocation of that supervisor's workload. How well did the plan work?

With a staff of three and the help of three temporary data entry operators we installed the system, completed the conversion and produced our first financial statements on the new system within 60 days. The system vendor told us that he had never seen an installation completed within 60 days much less during the height of the customer's season.

Construction Client - A client in the construction industry was having difficulty getting the billing out on time. In fact, the billing wasn't getting out until *three weeks* after the completion of the project.

Within a month after installing the **Making The Exceptional** Normal system, the client was able to cut the billing time from **three weeks** to **two days**. They were able to pay off their credit line and leave it untapped for four consecutive months saving $16,000 in interest.

If you agree that these are exceptional results, join me as we preview the **Making The Exceptional** Normal system.

3

System Overview

The key elements of the *Making The Exceptional Normal* system are:

The Plan - A set of *team* goals and priorities designed to assure that the most important work is accomplished first.

The Forum - A weekly meeting in which each member of the team has input in defining the goals and priorities that form the plan.

The Impetus – Describes the forces that drive exceptional performance. Included are steps for creating an environment that taps into your employees' natural motivations.

The Trust Factor - Reviews the key elements of trust and how they impact a person's willingness to go beyond what is normally expected of them.

Blending Goals – Describes how your willingness to blend your goals with those of your employees affects the results you get.

Measurements - Without measurable goals you cannot evaluate your team's performance. You will not know that you have produced exceptional results unless you have a standard against which to measure those results.

These are not menu items. You cannot choose which you want to employ. Later chapters will demonstrate why your team's ability to create exceptional results depends upon the application of all elements of the **Making The Exceptional** Normal system.

4

The Plan

Everyone agrees that having a plan is essential, as long as *someone else* does the planning. Most of us are "doers", not planners, as evidenced by the motto, "When all else fails read the directions". Even when someone else creates the plan (in the form of instructions), most of us won't take the time to read it.

Take a moment and think about how much time you would have saved over the years by simply following the instructions when assembling kids' toys, doing "basic" home repairs or learning a new piece of software. Now view that time as consecutive leisure hours. I'll bet you haven't had that much time off since high-school summer vacation.

Simply multiply that time savings by the number of people on your staff to get a sense for the magnitude of time savings and productivity increases you can expect from your plan.

Another advantage of planning is the *sense of control* it gives the planner. The inevitable "surprises" that rock your world are handled more quickly and with less stress when you evaluate them within the framework of your plan. Maintaining control while demands on your time increase exponentially will improve your health, happiness and long-term success.

Increased productivity, easy handling of surprises and stress reduction all become realities when you overcome your natural "doer" instincts and create a plan.

The reason that most of us avoid planning is that we view it as a laborious, solitary, time-consuming effort. It doesn't have to be that way. In fact, the greatest results come when plans are created by a group in less than two hours per week. In later chapters we will discuss simple techniques to deal with the less attractive aspects of planning, but first let's look at what the plan should include.

Key elements of a plan
There are really only two things that you and your staff need to consider when creating a plan:

- what work needs to get done (setting goals)
- in what sequence the work should be done (establishing priorities).

In the early stages, you will find that defining what needs to be done is easier than deciding upon the sequence in which to do the work. As time passes and your plan reduces the size of your staff's "to do" list, your attention will shift to the future and what direction you want your staff's efforts to take. For now, let's consider goal setting the easier of the two tasks and focus our attention on setting priorities.

The interesting thing about setting priorities is that we all bring different:

- backgrounds
- experiences
- knowledge
- views of the "big picture"
- work preferences
- skills

to bear when making priority decisions. Let's take a look at a few of these factors to see how they affect our decision-making process.

Experiences - An employee reprimanded for missing the deadline on a weekly report will almost certainly make that task a priority in the future, possibly at the cost of more important tasks.

Conversely, work assignments given without deadlines or accountability cause the employee to question the value of the work and may even result in important practices being neglected. Here's an example of how easily vital tasks can lose priority status.

A client's employee, who was responsible for posting productivity information on the shop bulletin board, became overwhelmed with her workload and forgot to update the bulletin board. No one questioned the omission. The next day, still struggling to gain ground, she again did not post the results. This went on for several more days at which time she decided to stop posting results since no one seemed concerned about the missing information.

As you might suspect the shop's productivity declined. It took three months for the lost productivity to show up as higher production costs in the client's financial statements. Only then did my client investigate and identify the missing information as the reason for declining productivity. A lesson learned the hard way.

When an employee consistently places a low-priority task near the top of his or her priority list, explore their experiences as a possible explanation. Here are a couple of non-threatening approaches you might use:

"This task is important, but I am wondering whether it should have a higher priority than tasks X or Y?"

or

"Is someone expecting this information (project) early in the week? If not, can we save it for later in the week?"

Differing views of the "big picture" - Where you are in the organization dictates the amount and type of information you have and how you set priorities.

A bookkeeper, facing a choice between completing a payroll tax return on time to avoid a penalty or performing an analysis for the sales department, will typically prepare the tax return. The likelihood of this choice does not diminish even when the bookkeeper knows that the sales department is waiting for information to submit a proposal for a *huge* contract. Why? Because they lack some or all of the following information:

- the deadline for the proposal
- what work the sales force needs to do once it gets the information

- how much time and money has been invested to get to this point
- what long-term impact this contract might have
- what the potential profit from this contract might be
- how the profit compares against the penalties for filing late

When we look at the missing information and add the likelihood that the bookkeeper will be severely chastised for causing the company to incur a penalty, it is easy to see why the decision is to prepare the tax return first.

When helping your employees establish priorities don't be afraid to ask them,

"What consequences do we face if this task is given a lower priority?"

Work preferences - As a manager, your reluctance to get involved in setting priorities opens the door for the employees to do first that which they enjoy the most. The result is that less savory (often more important) tasks are postponed.

This human frailty doesn't disappear when we become managers. We may strive harder than our staff members to overcome this tendency, but given a choice between doing something we enjoy and something we dislike, we usually opt for fun. How can we reasonably expect anything different from our employees?

When an employee inappropriately places a certain *type* of work low on the priority list, it may be a sign that they don't enjoy the work. While you can't allow employees to be selective about the type of work they do, realize that they are most productive when doing what they enjoy. The more often that you can match your employees' interests with their work, the more successful your team will be.

How can you determine whether an employee's reluctance to perform a task is related to their interest in the work? Offer two projects. The first project will be one that you *know* the person really enjoys. The second will be type of work to which the person has typically assigned a low priority. Then use the following verbiage to help uncover the reasons behind their choice:

"Just out of curiosity, what made you choose this project?"

or

"Why does this project have greater appeal to you than the other project?"

or

"You seem to have a greater interest in this type of work, what makes this interesting to you?"

Knowledge of what makes work "fun" for your employees can help you significantly increase your workforce's productivity.

Skills - Sometimes a project is "more fun" simply because the employee knows that he or she possesses the skills necessary to do the work. If a project never makes it to the top of the priority list, explore the possibility that the employee might be concerned about being able to do a good job.

When you suggest a completion date, don't just accept the "Yeah, yeah, no problem!" kind of response. Look for signs of uneasiness, the averted glance, hesitation in the voice or attempts to place less important tasks first. If these signs exist find a way to reopen the subject. Simple phrases like:

"It's been a while since we discussed the project, let's review what it is we are trying to accomplish."

or

"Let's review the key components of the project so that we don't overlook anything."

then add,

"If you have any questions we can answer them before you start the project".

The invitation to answer questions lets the employee know that it is all right to seek more information; that you *expect* questions to arise. This gives the employee the freedom to ask questions without feeling inept. You will gain greater cooperation and assure greater success from their effort with this approach.

If necessary, invest a little extra time guiding their efforts. This investment can reap huge dividends. The employee will acquire new knowledge, gain confidence and a greater appreciation of your interest in their growth.

Now that you have seen some of the factors that affect how people make priority decisions let's take a look at your role as manager in guiding those decisions.

How many of you provide any guidance at all? If you are honest with yourselves, most of you would have to admit that you don't do as good a job as you should. Often you assign a task without inquiring about the employee's workload or what other deadlines they face. Then you shake your head in dismay when the employee doesn't do the work in the sequence *you* envisioned. How do I know? Been there, done that.

Planning is the first element in the **Making The Exceptional** Normal system. A well thought out plan includes specific goals prioritized to ensure that the most important tasks are accomplished first. Successful implementation of the plan has the following advantages:

- better time utilization
- increased productivity
- greater ease in dealing
  with the unexpected
- less stress
- a sense of accomplishment

The means for assuring successful implementation will be discussed in the chapter 10, "The Initial Meeting" and chapter 11, "Subsequent Meetings", but first let's find a way to take the pain out of planning.

5

The Forum

In order to understand the significance of the forum you need to be aware of the following reality:

Any task, regardless of how unpleasant, becomes more palatable when others share the burden.

My wife and I are fortunate to have learned the advantages of shared effort. Whenever one of us faces a disagreeable task, something we really don't enjoy doing, the other will pitch in and help. The benefits are incredible:

- the task gets done more quickly
- the person responsible for the task maintains a positive attitude and pleasant demeanor

- the helper receives repeated demonstrations of appreciation
- the helper experiences personal satisfaction
- the bond between the parties becomes stronger

This simple concept, sharing the burden, when applied to the planning process, minimizes the natural aversion that both managers and staff have to planning.

SHARING THE BURDEN

There is no reason why you, as manager, should be responsible for setting every staff member's schedule. In fact, such an attempt usually creates resistance and resentment.

Most of the people you supervise truly care about the company's welfare. They view themselves as responsible, intelligent, motivated and insightful contributors to that welfare. Attempts to "control" their efforts are seen as indications that you either aren't aware of or don't respect those traits.

Yet, in the previous chapter, we saw some of the dangers of leaving employees to their own devices in setting priorities. How can we balance the employees' need for self-direction with our need to see the work accomplished in a certain sequence and within specified time frames? The key is the forum we choose and how we operate within that forum.

THE FORUM

A weekly staff meeting requiring less than 2 hours is all that is needed for the creation of an effective plan. During the weekly meeting *everyone is expected to set their own goals and priorities* for the coming week. A little skeptical? I would be too, but I have seen this approach work in so many different environments. The skills of the people involved ranged from whatever they had learned on the job to Masters Degree holders with significant work experience.

Let's see how well I can anticipate your questions about the use of a 2 hour weekly meeting format.

Why weekly?
There are several reasons:

> We think in terms of a "work week". Using a *natural* time frame simplifies the effort.

> Daily planning would leave us feeling that all we do is plan. Since most of us don't enjoy the effort, why subject ourselves to the pain?

> Another disadvantage of daily planning is the amount of time "lost" reanalyzing a workload that hasn't changed much from the previous day. A more enjoyable and gratifying use of that time is the accomplishment of tasks that reduce the size of your workload.

> Longer-term planning is appropriate for projects that for reasons of size, complexity or dependence upon others cannot be completed within a week. Often these projects lose priority status to projects with earlier deadlines. This can

have the effect of allowing less important work to be completed at the expense of a valuable long-term initiative.

One way to avoid this problem is to divide the larger projects into smaller increments that can be completed in a week. This assures that a component of the project is included in each week's goals and, thus, receives the attention is deserves.

Conversely, if you attempt to do longer-term planning for projects that can be completed in a few hours or days, you will find that your plans are usually thwarted. Why? Unanticipated workload additions as well as employees' personal issues like illness, baby-sitter availability and car problems tend to derail this approach to planning. The farther out you try to plan the more you expose yourself to these vagaries so why waste the time planning?

The most practical and effective planning time frame is a week.

Why tie up so many people?
The advantages of group dynamics are *incredible*. Here are some of the more significant benefits:

1) Shared vision - We spoke earlier of the problems associated with people not having enough information to make good priority decisions (the bookkeeper that opted to do the tax return before the sales department analysis).

I recently presented a financial seminar in which a participant's question resulted in a co-worker saying, "So that's why you are always bugging me for that report! From now on I'll make sure that you get it on time."

By sharing goals and priorities each member of the group has a clearer view of the "big picture" and how they fit into that picture which brings us to the second benefit.

2) Better coordination - When everyone sees the same picture it is easier for each member to set their goals and priorities to assure completion of the most important *group* goals.

Evidence of this will surface in a couple of different forms:

- a member realigning priorities to assure that a co-worker gets the information needed to complete an important project
- an individual foregoing some of his or her work to volunteer for a project

Lest you think these gestures too magnanimous, remember that we all want to be part of a winning effort.

3) Improved workload allocation - Regardless of how busy we think we are, planning will demonstrate that there is more than adequate time to do all the "important" work. It is true that we may not have time to do *everything*, but we have ample time to do what is of *greatest value.*

When we look at our schedules in terms of what is *important* and what would be *nice* to accomplish, we realize that some weeks will be lighter than others. A part of your job as manager is to ensure that the group is always focused on the most important tasks, those that will provide the greatest value to the company when completed.

If someone with a light week or low-priority tasks doesn't volunteer to forego their work to help someone with a hectic week or more beneficial goals, you will have to find a way to enlist their involvement. Usually asking them to assume some of a colleague's duties *and* to make those duties a priority in their schedules is all that it takes. Typically, they will have seen the value of the effort and simply need some prompting to "volunteer".

Notice that I said "asking" them. Even though everyone understands that you have the authority to require them to do the work, you will get better cooperation and less resentment if you ask them for their help rather than demand it.

Asking is a sign of respect which acknowledges the individual's desire to have input in deciding their role. It also credits them with the ability to make the right decisions and produce the desired results.

Another reason for "asking" instead of telling is to avoid the natural aversion we have to being told what to do. Our resistance to taking direction from others first manifests itself around the age of two. At that time we began the journey of asserting our independence and claiming control over our actions. We need only examine the lives of those closest to us to see the desire for independence grow over time.

4) Workforce flexibility - As staff members help each other with their workloads they will gain knowledge, skills and procedural understanding about each other's work. Your staff will become *cross-trained*. This adds tremendous versatility to your workforce and enormous contingency options to your planning effort.

Cross-training offers protection from the vagaries of illness and personal demands on your employees' time. It positions your group to produce *exceptional* results.

Equally important is that cross training is accomplished without the employees perceiving a threat to their job security. Why? Because:

- the effort isn't viewed as cross training; it is movement toward a goal
- *they* initiated or were a party to the decision
- they understand the motives for shifting the workload

5) Team spirit - Watch any winning sports team at the final buzzer and what do you see? Players racing toward each other to share the joy and congratulate one another. Why? Because there is no lonelier feeling than being happy and having no one with whom to share that happiness.

Your team doesn't have to play sports to experience these same emotions. Anytime a group of people successfully combine their efforts to achieve a goal, overcome an obstacle or solve a problem, all members of the team experience wonderful feelings of:

- personal value or worth
- satisfaction with a job done well
- appreciation for the contributions of others.

Think back to one of *your* team experiences. It doesn't have to be related to business; any successful group endeavor will do. What did the group achieve? Do you remember the feelings you had when the dream became a reality? I'll bet you can actually *feel* those same emotions today, years after your team's success.

The powerful memories and natural highs that come from successful efforts leave everyone wanting more. Team spirit is a natural byproduct of the joy and satisfaction of successful team efforts. Use your staff's success and the team spirit it creates to assure exceptional results in your team's future.

6) Better solutions - Problem-solving approaches are as unique as the individuals attacking the problem. If you doubt this statement, try a simple test. Give five people the same problem and limit the time for its solution to a few minutes. Make sure that the problem would normally require *more* than the allotted time.

When the time is up ask each of them to describe step by step, the approach they used in identifying the source of the problem, how far along they had gotten in developing a solution and what they intended to do next. See the differences?

Now ask them *why* they chose that approach. What did you learn? How did differences in education, experience, innate abilities and involvement in similar problem-solving situations influence the way in which each of them saw the problem? How did it impact their approach to its solution?

Tap into those diverse backgrounds, experiences and abilities to find better (and probably quicker) solutions to the challenges facing your staff.

7) Improvement opportunities - As you and your staff establish the next week's goals and priorities, it is inevitable that you will want to accomplish more than your staff feels is realistically possible. If used properly this apparent conflict can become the catalyst for improvement. "There just isn't enough time" is your springboard to greater productivity.

Before we discuss how to make this leap, let's review some do's and don'ts that will impact your ability to get them to stretch beyond their comfort zones.

DO:

- Make sure that every employee knows that you view inefficiencies as system problems and not performance problems
- Ask them to estimate the time required for each task on their list
- When a task appears to take longer to perform than seems reasonable ask, "What is it that requires so much time?" (this verbiage reinforces your earlier statement that you view all problems as system problems)
- Solicit the help of others in the group to find less time-consuming approaches to completing the task
- State your belief that they have the intelligence and creativity to find a better way to perform the task

- Pay close attention to employees' concerns
- Gain consensus on an alternative that will save time
- Implement the change immediately
- Recognize the contributors for their insights
- Add additional tasks to the priority list

DON'T:

- Use language that assigns blame
- Question the ability of an employee in the presence of others
- Question an employee's motives in front of others
- Verbalize doubts about an employee's ability to do the job
- Ignore the employee's concerns about an alternative solution
- Create opportunities for failure

These simple rules will allow you to explore the reasons why they feel they don't have enough time for all the things you want to accomplish without creating conflict. In some instances their concerns will be well-founded and you must acknowledge your oversight. In other situations you will be able to demonstrate that there are needless tasks that can be eliminated or less time-consuming approaches that can be employed which will allow the accomplishment of all of the goals you had envisioned.

When you demonstrate interest in their perspectives and a willingness to admit the validity of their concerns, you gain their respect. The consideration sown will create a harvest of willing cooperation. They *will* help you find approaches to improving the team's performance.

Don't miss the opportunity to achieve stretch goals. Employ the simple techniques just outlined to lead your team to exceptional performance.

What size group?
Typically, the meeting should include no more than six to eight participants.

If your department is large enough to have another layer of management between you and the staff, limit the participants in your meeting to those who report directly to you, but no more than eight people. Then have each of them hold a similar meeting with their staff members.

In situations where everyone in the department reports to you divide the department into manageable groups and have a separate meeting with each group. The purpose of the small group size is to allow the meetings to move more quickly and to increase the level of participation. Some people aren't comfortable voicing their opinions in large groups. Don't lose their valuable insights by creating an uncomfortable environment.

How do the employees feel about this approach?
I recently returned from a client that had been using this approach successfully for about six months. That's right, I said "had". Three months ago this husband and wife team decided that they wanted to give their children more parental attention. The wife wanted to spend more time

with the children and, when her husband readily agreed, she discontinued her involvement in the business.

The wife had installed the **Making The Exceptional** Normal system for the administrative group. In her absence the weekly meeting died a natural death. During a recent meeting with the administrative group, they expressed concern that they no longer had a clear picture of where they were and what was most important. They missed the sense of direction they had enjoyed in earlier weekly meetings.

The group was polled and without exception they agreed that the meetings should be reinstated. One of the senior members of the group volunteered to lead the weekly meetings. *Wait! It gets better.*

As soon as the procedural arrangements were completed, the group began to discuss problems in the field operations. They quickly identified a half dozen improvement opportunities. We discussed some simple reporting formats that would highlight the problem areas. They then agreed to find time in their schedules to provide weekly reports to field operations management so that *they too* could focus on the most important tasks. I could not develop an argument more compelling than this experience.

Employees want more control over their activities. They find comfort in knowing where they are and where they are headed. They gain satisfaction from finding better ways to do things. They enjoy being productive. Make sure that these enjoyable aspects exist in their jobs and they will reward you with exceptional results.

A weekly meeting requiring less than 2 hours will allow you to:

- make planning fun
- assure that all team members have goals for the coming week
- establish priorities for those goals
- create a shared vision
- give employees a sense for how they fit into the "big picture"
- identify system inefficiencies (needless work and time-consuming approaches)
- give employees the satisfaction of determining their own plans
- establish accountability for results
- create an opportunity for them to experience more enjoyment in their jobs than they have experienced in quite some time

6

The Impetus

What are the forces that drive *exceptional* performance? Why are employees willing to participate in these efforts? Why, as in the case of my client's employees, did they feel compelled to reinstate and *expand* those efforts?

In our discussion of planning and the weekly meeting format we uncovered the following motivators:

- control over their activities
- comfort in knowing where they are and where they are headed
- satisfaction of finding better ways to do things
- the joy of being productive

But these motivators represent only part of the explanation. Let's take a look at some of the other *powerful* forces that will keep you and your staff ever vigilant in your search for greater productivity.

Peer Pressure - Unfortunately this phrase carries a negative connotation. Its most common use relates to teenagers being subjected to negative influences. The reality is that everyone experiences peer pressure, but as we mature we are less likely to permit this pressure to influence our value system. Now let's take a look at how peer pressure works to make our lives as managers easier.

One characteristic of our humanity is the desire to avoid what we don't enjoy. It is easy for us to find other things to do when we are facing a task we don't like. Left on our own we may delude ourselves into thinking that we are doing important work.

One of the advantages of the group meeting is that it becomes more difficult to allow ourselves this deception. In a group environment, we are concerned about what our co-workers think of us. When we examine our goals and priorities through their eyes we are more honest in our assessment of what really constitutes important work.

Since our colleagues work in close proximity to us they also realize how long it takes us to do various tasks. If we are tempted to fudge on the time required to do a given task, we run the risk of having our co-workers see through our smoke screen; an embarrassing prospect that we typically won't invite. Most of us find performing unpleasant tasks less distasteful than being embarrassed in front of our co-workers.

One caveat, don't try to *use* peer pressure. Simply allow it to work for you. It is neither a weapon for whipping your staff into shape, nor a tool for fixing performance problems. It *is* a natural byproduct of group dynamics that produces results.

Any attempts to tinker with peer pressure will be obvious. Employees will view your efforts as manipulative. You will lose credibility AND their support. The possibility of exceptional results will become as remote as the dream in chapter one.

Variety - How do you feel when you have to do the same task over and over and over and over again? Do you get a little bored? I'll bet you were getting bored just reading the "over"s in the first sentence.

Boredom is a terrible thing. It wastes valuable time and resources. When bored, we:

- take more frequent breaks
- do more daydreaming
- spend time bemoaning our plight (mentally to ourselves or, worse yet, verbally to others - now we're tying up at least two people's time and talents)

This reality explains why it takes more time to complete boring tasks than those we enjoy. As if that weren't bad enough, our mental flights from boredom cause us to make more mistakes. Now, we not only get to experience the embarrassment and frustration of a "dumb" mistake, we get to do the same boring task all over again. Isn't life grand?

It can be *if* we remember that everyone needs variety and we build variety into everyone's work. No, I don't mean that every task has to be new and exciting. But each week's activities should include duties that allow every employee to experience something different.

Variety comes in many forms. It can be as simple as:

- adding a new dimension to any effort
- shifting work from one employee to another
- having employees review processes to find more effective approaches to doing the work
- having employees trade tasks
- asking employees to find ways to build additional benefits into an effort

One approach that always worked well for me was the special project. I maintained a list of projects that I wanted to complete. During the weekly meeting I made my staff aware of these projects and my need for their assistance. The only prerequisite for involvement in a special project was that the individual had to have completed **all** of the priority goals on their list.

Wait a minute, Dale! Are you saying that if I offer my staff variety they will work more quickly to complete their tasks so that they can take on more work? That is exactly what I am saying. Before you dismiss this concept as the mad ravings of a lunatic, there are three things I would like you to do.

First, think back to a time when you were involved in a boring task and someone asked you for help *when you completed your task.* How did you react? Did your focus on the current task intensify? Was the work accomplished with greater ease? Did the task seem to get done more quickly? Sure, it did. Why? Because avoidance is a powerful motivator and you wanted to avoid the boredom you were experiencing.

Second, remember a time when you asked an employee, one involved in a boring task, to help with a new project. What reaction did you get? Did the person's posture become more erect? Were they anxious to attack the new task? Was their behavior more animated? Did a sense of excitement develop? Did their attention to the work become more focused, more intense than when you initiated the discussion? The answer to all of these is a resounding YES!

Finally, try the special project approach with several of your employees. Pay particular attention to their behavior as you assign them a project. Notice their physical responses. Are they as described in the preceding paragraph? I am certain that you will find their reactions indicate a renewed level of interest, excitement and desire to get started as quickly as possible.

Build variety into your staff's work and they will reward you with exceptional performance.

Challenge - Some of the most vivid and satisfying memories we have are of times when we stretched and accomplished more than we ever thought possible. Why? The completion of the task represents victory over our fears and self-doubt which, in turn, changes our self image. After successfully handling any new challenge we view ourselves as confident, capable people who, having mastered our fears, can accomplish anything we choose.

These feelings are powerful motivators, but those of us in management seldom tap into that power to help our employees become more productive. Rather we tend to keep the more challenging work for ourselves. Why? Because it's less *boring*.

Another reason for not assigning challenging work to our employees is an arrogance born in our subconscious mind. When we become managers we see ourselves as different, possibly better than our employees. This attitude is reinforced when we notice that our employees don't pursue variety and challenge as aggressively as we do. The result is that we don't assign challenging work to them.

What should you do? Challenge your employees on a weekly basis. Monitor their behavior. You will find that their confidence rises, they smile more frequently and they demonstrate a desire for more new challenges.

Still skeptical? Think about any child you know, one of your own, a niece or nephew, or a friend's child. Remember one of their recent accomplishments. Did they learn to ride a bike, master a new game, read or solve a math problem? What reactions did you observe? Were they smiling with a sense of pride? Did their speech become more animated and seemingly endless? Was the confidence level elevated? Were they anxious to return and repeat the success? Of course they were.

Satisfaction associated with overcoming challenges is universal. The question is, "How do we create challenges that tap into our employees' natural motivation?".

First, we must remember that there can be no satisfaction without success. If we challenge our employees beyond their capabilities we create failure. Failure causes them to withdraw from future challenges. While the possibility exists that we may inadvertently invite failure, the danger of this happening isn't as great as we believe.

We are more likely to underestimate their abilities and fall short of providing a worthwhile challenge than overly challenging them. Why? Two reasons. The more obvious is that if they fail it will reflect poorly on us. The second relates to a subconscious arrogance that simply says the task is too complex for them.

I hope to debunk that myth with the following personal experience. I was controller of a mortgage banking operation and had a rather complicated special project awaiting someone's time. The first person available to do the work was a woman in her early fifties whose background consisted of what she had learned on the job.

Frankly, I was reluctant to assign her the project because I didn't feel that she could handle it. Fortunately, I resisted the temptation.

We spent an extra twenty minutes reviewing the project because I wanted to be certain that she understood what I was trying to accomplish, why it was important, what benefit it would have to the company and how to approach the task. As she left my office, I couldn't help but wonder whether I had made a serious mistake.

An hour later she came back into my office and said, "Dale, there is one type of transaction that I keep running into that we didn't discuss. I think it is going to have a significant impact on your analysis, do you have time to discuss it now?". When we reviewed her findings I couldn't believe that I had overlooked something so major. *Significant impact* was an understatement. I would have come to an erroneous conclusion had she not realized my oversight.

This woman, whose abilities that I had seriously doubted, pulled my bacon out of the fire. This occurred over twenty years ago. If that doesn't give you a sense for the magnitude of my oversight, I don't know what will.

She taught me to trust people when they say they can do the job. It isn't a blind trust. I set mechanisms in place for periodic reviews, interim goals or other safety devices, but I no longer prejudge the employee's abilities.

Don't deprive your employees of the satisfaction, confidence and sense of worth that they gain from these experiences. Create new challenges for them and your efforts will be rewarded with exceptional results.

Learning - When we think of learning we typically picture a classroom environment, but the opportunities for learning transcend these formal structures. Variety and challenge create natural learning experiences. By simply satisfying these two needs we provide our employees with opportunities to learn.

Why is learning important? The need to learn is closely tied to our self image. When we learn we view ourselves as having greater value and rightfully so. Our newly acquired knowledge equips us to handle future challenges more effectively. We gain confidence which allows us to more quickly overcome our fears and self-doubts enabling us to accept challenges more readily.

We also acquire the confidence to help others. When someone seeks counsel from us, our belief that we have value is affirmed. This sense of value drives the desire to learn more, to become even more valuable. This renewed interest in learning forms the basis for skill development essential to your staff's ability to consistently produce exceptional results.

Growth - At one time or another during our lives we have had the feeling that no matter how hard we tried, how much effort we put forth, we simply weren't making any headway.

Remember how depressing that experience was? Did you begin to question whether the goal was worth the effort? Were you tempted to give up? Were there any instances where you did abandon the effort? How did that impact your approach to other goals you had?

When people don't experience personal growth they become depressed. The longer the depression lasts the more likely they are to give up. This simple truth explains why we so often see "retirement on the job". Lack of personal and professional growth opportunities may not be the only explanation, but it is a significant contributor to the problem. The related productivity losses are enormous.

As managers, we have both the opportunity and responsibility to see that our employees aren't among those who have "retired on the job." Many bright, talented people have longed for growth in their jobs only to have those desires thwarted by limited duties and mundane tasks. Eventually they gave up hope of experiencing that growth and quit its pursuit.

Those of us in management positions find it difficult to understand why others give up. After all, we had supervisors and managers who tried to thwart our efforts and we didn't let it happen. Why have others allowed this to happen to them?

One explanation is that we don't all value career in the same way. Those of us who aspire to management roles place greater value on our careers. In the process we give up other aspects of our lives. Hopefully these were conscious decisions so that we haven't become distressed over not "having it all".

Employees who don't aspire to management positions typically place greater value on the family, leisure activities or community service than on their careers. These are life style choices that need to be understood and respected. I doubt that any of us fortunate enough to live in the U.S. would question the right of each individual to make his or her own life style choices.

Another explanation could be the environment in which the individual grew up. Some people do not receive encouragement during their attempts to grow which make it difficult for them to persist when "at first they don't succeed".

Others are taught that aggressiveness is not an attractive trait, that they should just do a good job and they will eventually be recognized for their efforts. A nice ideal that seldom produces the desired result.

In the most debilitating environment the individual is told that he or she is not bright or talented. The person is told that he or she will never accomplish much. If repeated frequently enough and over a long enough period of time, the message creates an image of powerlessness that the individual finds almost impossible to overcome.

Growth experiences counteract these feelings of futility and the attendant attitudes of disinterest, low self-image and diminished value.

Think about a time in your life when you were successful in improving your abilities. Any experience will do; it doesn't have to relate to business. Maybe you were trying to become a more patient parent, trying to improve your golf score or simply being a better friend.

Whatever your growth expectation, you persisted and your efforts paid off. How did you feel? Were you depressed? Did you wonder why you bothered? Did you question whether it was worth the effort? Did you vow that you would never again embark on a path for growth? Absolutely not!

You felt *alive, vital, confident, proud, energized* and ready to repeat the experience so that you could, once again, feel the satisfaction associated with personal growth.

Our employees share our need for growth. They may not be as aggressive in their attempts to satisfy this need, but that doesn't alter the fact that the need exists. As managers it is our job to provide employees with opportunities for growth.

Provide variety, challenge and learning opportunities for your employees and you automatically create an environment that promotes their growth.

Even those who have been conditioned to believe that they possess few skills and little talent, can regain the natural desire to grow. It takes only one success to rekindle the flame. The key is to create challenges well within the individual's capability. This approach **assures** their success. If done properly, the employee feels that he or she is stretching, while you bask in the knowledge that they will succeed.

Expect resistance to your initial attempts, but don't cave into that resistance. It is important that you genuinely believe that they can succeed (not too hard when you structure the challenge). Then state emphatically your confidence in their ability to be successful and your trust that they will do a good job

Most people don't want to disappoint others. Specifically, they don't want to diminish the impression others have of them. Your statements of trust and confidence will increase their commitment to proving you right. The additional effort they put forth will assure their success. With each subsequent success their:

- confidence builds
- self-esteem grows
- desire for learning and growth is rekindled
- willingness to take on new challenges increases

What does this do for you? In addition to feeling great about having made another's life more enjoyable, you will open the spigot to a huge reservoir of skills and talent.

Peer pressure, variety, challenge, learning and growth are the impetus, the forces that drive exceptional performance. Another advantage of these powerful motivators is that they are *free* to anyone who chooses to employ them. When was the last time you were offered a solution that didn't take a chunk out of your budget?

7

The Trust Factor

How do you react to people you don't trust? Avoidance? "I won't deal with anyone I can't trust!"

But what if you don't have a choice? What if that person is your boss or a colleague? Most of us have fantasized about firing just such a person, but we *know* that will never happen. So what do we do? We find ways to **protect ourselves**.

We include others in our meetings to witness the events. If we can't justify a meeting we discuss issues and concepts with others <u>before</u> we communicate with the person whose approval we need. "I just wanted to bounce this idea off you before I go to the boss" can mean "I want to make sure that someone else knows that this is my idea so that the boss doesn't steal it".

We spend countless hours trying to determine how the distrusted person is going to hurt us, then we spend even more time trying to make certain that it doesn't happen. The productivity loss is huge.

Exceptional results cannot be sustained in an environment marked by distrust. Employees cannot simultaneously devote time and energy to protecting themselves and increasing productivity. It isn't physically possible. This truth leads to two obvious questions, "How do I gain my employees' trust?" and "What is it that they must trust?".

HOW DO I GAIN THEIR TRUST?
The way to gain anyone's trust is simply to be honest in all of your dealings with them. Very simply that translates into:

- don't say what you don't believe (integrity)
- don't promise what you can't deliver (promises)

Integrity - If you say things that you don't believe, the lack of enthusiasm in your voice, the hesitation in your speech, the failure to make eye contact and numerous other body language messages will override your words.

Anytime the listener senses that you are lying to them or withholding parts of the truth you have lost. You've lost their respect, confidence, trust, support and effort. These are heavy prices to pay. What makes these penalties even more severe is that you may never be able to recoup their trust. The old adage, "it takes a lifetime to develop a good reputation, two seconds to lose it" demonstrates the magnitude of the risk we take when we aren't honest in *all* of our dealings.

Promises - "We live in a reciprocal world", "You reap what you sow", and "What goes around comes around" all apply to promises. If you honor your commitments to others they are more inclined to honor theirs to you. Failure to keep your promises invites them to keep theirs only when it is *convenient* for them.

Exceptional performance cannot be achieved without your employees' commitment to the goals and priorities they helped establish. If you want them to live up to these commitments, you must honor yours.

Before we leave the topic of promises I want you to realize that making a promise isn't the same as guaranteeing results. If you aren't certain that you can deliver the result, you can still *promise to try*. Let's see how I employed "the promise to try" to prevent a mutiny.

Mutiny avoided
Do you remember the mortgage banking example where sixteen people were each working ten hours of overtime per week?

I quickly discovered that most of the overtime was being worked simply because the people wanted the extra income. I knew that if I just eliminated all the overtime and didn't offer them something in return I was likely to have a mutiny on my hands.

The mutiny would come in one of two forms. Either I would trigger a mass exodus (which would cost me my job) or they would stay and look for ways to prove me an inept manager (which would also cost me my job).

To further complicate matters, I didn't have the authority to increase salaries. In order to get *anyone* a raise, three things had to occur:

- the supervisor (me) had to provide a solid recommendation
- the department had to have an adequate budget to cover the increases
- a majority of the personnel committee had to vote for the increase

What I offered was a promise to *try* to get their salaries to the level they were getting with overtime. I explained that in order for me to have any chance of success they were going to have to provide me with ammunition to take to the personnel committee. Ammunition would have to take the form of exceptional results; something I could point to as having real value to support my request for higher salaries.

I could not promise them raises, but I could promise to *try*. I repeatedly made this distinction so that everyone understood I was being honest about what I could do. This honesty, coupled with all of the other elements of the **Making The Exceptional** Normal system enabled us to exceed the aggressive goals we had set.

We achieved our goals despite the loss of four full-time employees. The salary savings from these four employees gave me the budget necessary to provide the desired increases AND provide a net savings to the company. As you might imagine, the personnel committee was easily persuaded to approve salary increases for my staff.

People know when you are being honest with them. These folks knew that I couldn't promise them raises. If I had been foolish enough to make such a promise they wouldn't have believed me. Their commitment to our goals, if given at all, would have been as hollow as my promise of raises. This experience provides compelling evidence for the power of trust and its necessity for producing *exceptional* results.

WHAT IS IT THAT THEY MUST TRUST?

Do honesty and promise-keeping represent all that our employees expect from us to gain and hold their trust? Are there other behaviors they require before they *fully* trust us? The answers lie in your own experiences. How was your trust in another affected when he or she:

- spoke of your inadequacies to your colleagues
- criticized you publicly
- postponed discussions about your behavior or performance until a major problem arose
- withheld information critical to your success
- came across as a "know-it-all"
- demeaned your skills or experience
- gave others preferential treatment
- took credit for your work

I doubt that many of you would be willing to place much trust in that person again. Your employees' trust is dependent upon your ability to demonstrate that you:

- have their best interest at heart
- strive to help them become more successful
- listen to their concerns and help them deal with those concerns
- initially view all problems as system problems, not performance problems

- frame criticism in the context of personal improvement
- keep discussions about inappropriate behavior and poor performance private
- are open and receptive to their ideas
- recognize that you don't always have the best solution
- admit when you are wrong
- recognize them for a job well done
- thank them for their efforts

First and foremost, be *genuine* in these attitudes and beliefs. If your employees ever get the feeling that your efforts are designed to manipulate them, that you really aren't as concerned about them as you are the results, they will withdraw their trust and prevent the results you desire.

Trust, an essential component to exceptional results, can only be gained through genuine interest in the welfare of your employees.

8

Blending goals

"I want some candy. Mommy, I WANT SOME CANDY. MOMMYYYY, I WANT SOME CANDY!" We have all been around a child during one of these periods in which he or she demands satisfaction. Everyone in the area is annoyed by the child's behavior.

The *demanding* tone of the request puts us off. We can understand the child's desire for candy, but we have little tolerance for the demands being made upon the parent. Yet, how often do we, as managers, go to our employees and say, *"I need this report by 4 o'clock."*?

True, our tone is more civil, but we are still making *demands* on their time and energy. The fact that we aren't screaming offers little solace from the sting of being told what to do.

To further compound this personal slight, we overlook all previous instructions and deadlines given them. Then chastise them when the work isn't accomplished in the sequence we want.

How willingly would you go the extra mile for someone who treats you in the manner just described? You need only remember similar treatment from one of your managers for the answer to that question.

Leading your employees to exceptional results requires that you avoid the seemingly "natural" approach of making demands. Let's take a look at an alternative approach.

Natural conflict
There will always be a natural conflict between your growth goals and the tasks your employees *must* perform. If you want your employees to achieve the growth goals, you must respect what they have to do and help them find ways to complete those tasks more quickly. Let's look at what's involved in accomplishing this feat. During your weekly meeting:

- make your wishes known up front; state the benefits to be gained from each effort
- remind them that they can put a little variety in their work by becoming involved in these new efforts
- state, unequivocally, that you would *like* to blend as many of these items into next week's schedule as possible

- ask each employee to review his or her goals and priorities for the coming week in light of this wish list (most employees will subordinate tasks on their lists to those on your wish list that have greater value)
- set interim (weekly) goals for longer-term projects to assure that the final deadline isn't missed
- achieve group consensus on the plan
- express, **sincerely**, your appreciation for both their willingness to find ways to accomplish *exceptional* results and their skilled evaluation of what is important

This simple approach delivers the following messages to your employees:

- you understand that they face challenges with their existing workload
- you won't have a complete picture of what needs to be done until you hear their plans
- your wishes aren't always top priority; you recognize that there are times when the mandatory tasks must take precedence over growth goals
- you are interested in their ideas and insights
- you appreciate their efforts in finding ways to accomplish more
- you realize that they are adults capable of making intelligent decisions

The respect and consideration implicit in these messages indicate that you truly care about your employees. How do you respond to someone who gives you respect, who considers your needs, who wants to be a part of your solution rather than the source of your problems? Most of us reflect the same consideration back to the giver.

If you want *exceptional* results *don't demand* that your goals always be given priority status, *blend* them with those of your employees.

9

Measurements

Up to this point our efforts have centered around finding ways to set goals and priorities so that the most important tasks are accomplished first. We haven't yet discussed how to determine which tasks are most important. There is both art and science involved in making that determination.

ART
Devising performance measures that provide guidance in establishing and prioritizing goals is the *art* component. There are no hard, fast rules to follow. No trail to guide to the one and only set of measures we will ever need. It isn't possible because needs change with each success. Even within a specific goal we may need different measures at various stages of movement toward that goal.

Think of your goals as a "to do" list. As you complete an item on the list your focus changes to the next item. The skills and resources needed to accomplish the next task will be different than the one just completed and so will the way in which you measure success.

Each success requires the establishment of new goals, new approaches to achieving those goals and new measures of success. This is the natural pattern of growth. Just as a plant drops leaves to support new growth we must drop old measures to promote our growth to higher levels of success. By understanding this process we can avoid getting comfortable with and hanging onto measures that no longer work.

SCIENCE
Science becomes important when tracking and reporting systems are established to monitor performance. The key to successful system development is simplicity. All too often we invest huge sums of time, effort and money into developing elaborate systems. There are several problems associated with this approach:

- We ignore the fact that these measures have to change. Elaborate systems usually don't allow measures to be revised quickly.

- System development and implementation often take longer than goal actualization would have taken.

- We become so enamored with tracking a wide array of information that we lose sight of those few measures that are critical to our success.

- We hang onto our measures long after they have outlived their usefulness because we don't want to go through the pain of another major system overhaul.

Let's take a look at some simple measures that produced *exceptional* results.

EXAMPLES
Construction client
Remember the client who reduced billing time from three weeks to two days? There were actually three goals they wanted to achieve. They wanted to:

- reduce the time it took to get the billing out
- use the additional cash to pay down the credit line
- improve their response time on requests for proposal

The following information was reported in an $8^{1/2}$" by 14" format:

Billing
- job number
- completion date
- billing date

Cash Position
- cash on hand
- anticipated accounts receivable collections for the week
- anticipated cash expenditures for the week
- cash improvement or shortfall for the week

Proposals
- customer name and phone number
- date of request for proposal
- date proposal was sent
- estimated start date for the job

This brief report allowed the team to see at a glance where they were making improvements and where they were falling short of expectations. It kept their attention focused on the most important goals. The increased focus assured priority status for these efforts in the planning process.

Another advantage of this report is that it highlights individual failings without rendering judgment or making inflammatory comments about that individual's performance. It simply states the facts.

This is where peer pressure begins to work for you. The discomfort of having fellow workers see their failings motivates the person to perform better. Usually the individual's performance improves without you having to utter a word. I'll bet you never dreamed that avoiding confrontation could be so easy.

Heating and air-conditioning client
This client complained that no matter how hard he tried he couldn't get a handle on what was going on in his business.

Was the **Making The Exceptional** Normal system able to help him? This is how he answered that question, "In two hours a week, I now learn more about what's going on in my organization than I used to learn in a whole week". What measures did we track that allowed him to exert greater control over his operations?

Service
- billable versus non-billable time by service person
- percentage of billable time to total time for service group
- number of installations
- comparison of actual versus budgeted time on installations
- number of callbacks versus calls handled

Financial
- installations jobs sold with projected profit margins by sales person
- comparison of actual versus projected profits on jobs completed during the week
- inventory levels and turnover rates
- cash, receivables and payables status
- weekly cash flow projections for coming month
- revenue generated versus budget

Sales
- number of calls made and close rate
- comparison projected profit margins on jobs sold versus margin targets
- comparison of sales mix to company goals

These are just a few examples of the measures to be considered when establishing goals and priorities.

Measures should be defined by the company's current situation and its growth goals. If we were to establish measures for two heating and air-conditioning companies we might use similar measures. But if one has great profit margins but poor service delivery and the other has great delivery and poor pricing, the focus of our attention (the measures that we spend the most time improving) will be dramatically different.

When establishing measures consider:

- what it is that you want to accomplish
- where your team needs to focus its attention to achieve those goals
- how you will know whether or not they are successful

then

- convert those success indicators into performance measures
- create a report format that focuses on those measures
- watch how quickly *exceptional* results appear

10

The Initial Meeting

You are now ready to embark on a voyage that will leave in its wake, one *exceptional* result after another. Your ability to lead others to consistently higher levels of performance will gain you the respect of senior managers, peers and employees throughout the organization.

Here's an example of the type of reputation you can achieve. During my years with a national CPA firm, I did work for a client that was involved in fireproofing and drywalling commercial buildings. This firm had a project superintendent whose primary responsibility was to coordinate the work of several union groups, a daunting task to say the least.

MAKING THE EXCEPTIONAL NORMAL

This superintendent had a nickname, No Problem. Anytime he was asked to accomplish something out of the ordinary his response was "No problem!" He always delivered on his promises.

Everyone associated with this company, customers, vendors, peers, employees and even the owner of the business commented regularly on this man's ability to make the most difficult task look easy.

When you employ the **Making The Exceptional** Normal system you, too, will make the achievement of *exceptional* results seem effortless. In doing so you will gain the respect of all who have the privilege of working with you.

I don't want to mislead you. There is work involved in employing the tools described in this book, but the work is more enjoyable.

If we analyze our feelings toward work, we find that it isn't the work we mind, rather it is the lack of results that make the work unfulfilling.

Think back to a time when some of your work didn't accomplish what you had hoped. Remember the feelings? Frustration, disappointment and despair were your companions.

Now remember a time when your efforts really paid off. What did you feel? Elation, a sense of accomplishment and a desire to accomplish more were your sidekicks. You get to choose the company you keep. Choose wisely.

The initial meeting outline below is designed to help make the work *easier than you think and more fun than you can imagine.*

PREPARATION
Step One - Call your employees together. Let them know that you intend, with their help, to install a new system that will help alleviate stress in all of your jobs. *Ask* each of them to prepare a list of the tasks they need to complete for the coming week. Emphasize that no task is too small for inclusion on the list. Then, *ask* them to prioritize those tasks before the meeting. Finally, schedule the meeting.

Hopefully, you noticed the emphasis placed on the word "ask" in the last paragraph. Remember our earlier discussion of how different the reactions are when we ask for our employees' help rather than telling them what we want. Don't overlook this powerful tool when running your weekly meetings.

Step Two - Create a list of the things that you want to see accomplished. These are the growth goals that need to be blended with your staff's goals during the weekly meeting.

Step Three - Establish performance measures to help you prioritize the goals in step two. Goals with the greatest benefit for your *company* should be given highest priority. These may not always coincide with the goals that interest you most, but don't give into temptation. If you do, you can expect the following consequences.

Your staff will assume that since you don't have to work on the most important tasks first they don't either. When everyone shifts their attention from what is truly important to what they want to do the possibility of exceptional results and the attendant recognition quickly evaporate.

One of the beauties of the **Making The Exceptional** Normal system is that you never lose sight of your goals. The fact that you have to assign a low priority to a goal that interests you *doesn't* mean that you are giving up on that goal. You are simply postponing it to a future date.

This distinction is important because it allows you to avoid the frustration that accompanies not being able to do what we want. Why? Two reasons.

First, the sense of accomplishment that you and your staff gain from producing exceptional results will more than offset the disappointment of having postponed a goal.

Second, your team will have made a <u>conscious</u> decision to place one goal over another. To understand the importance of using the conscious rather than the subconscious mind when making decisions, let's explore the impact that each has on motivation.

The problem with allowing a decision to be made in the <u>subconscious</u> mind is the lack of *awareness* that a decision has been made. Consequently, the unachieved goals appear to have been "lost". When your subconscious repeatedly allows other tasks to take precedence over what you truly want, you give up hope that the goal will ever be achieved. Your despair causes you to look at every future goal as another opportunity for disappointment until you simply quit trying.

Conversely, use of the conscious mind provides:

- a sense of control over the results you achieve
- an awareness that you have given up *nothing*; rather you have postponed the satisfaction of one goal for achievement of another having greater benefit to you and your company
- knowledge of what is possible
- ideas for making more of what you want possible

In fact, the desire to get to more interesting goals can serve as an effective carrot in helping you move more quickly through the higher priority goals.

Conscious priority decisions allow you and your staff to make better choices while maintaining awareness of future goals.

Step Four - Review the factors essential to collaboration. We discussed motivators common to all employees including the ability to control their own activities and their desires for variety, challenge, learning and growth.

Our discussion of group dynamics demonstrated that avoidance is a powerful motivator. Not wanting to embarrass themselves in front of their peers causes the employees to make better goal and priority decisions.

On a more positive note, employees gain tremendous satisfaction from helping others, being asked to share their successes in a group setting and being recognized by their peers for ideas that improve the team's success.

All of these motivating factors can be capsulized by the acronym WIIFT (what's in it for them). What drives the success of the **Making The Exceptional** Normal program is simply paying attention to your employees' needs.

When you demonstrate your interest in assuring that their needs are met, when your actions show that your goals are not *always* more important than theirs, when you acknowledge that you don't have all the answers by asking for their input, you show them respect.

How do you respond to people who show you respect - who place their trust and confidence in you? Do you ignore the compliment or do you work to protect and enhance their perception of you? It is our nature to look to others for affirmation that we are bright, capable, trustworthy and deserving of respect. We work hard not to disappoint those who attribute these characteristics to us.

You will discover that by demonstrating your *genuine* belief that your employees possess these attributes you will gain more than their cooperation, you will get their initiative. They will find ways to demonstrate that they are better than the already favorable view you have of them.

Your repeated demonstration of concern for your employees will be repaid in kind. Whenever they can return the favor they will. I remember one instance where a client's employees called me in advance of my appointment to alert me to my client's ill humor. Why? I consistently demonstrated a concern for their needs and they wanted to repay the kindness.

A genuinely collaborative effort focused on goal and priority setting is the foundation for *exceptional* results.

THE MEETING

Step One - Start on time. Unless you are willing to make the meeting a priority in your schedule your employees will consider it another time-wasting demonstration of power.

Similarly, allowing people to trickle in late gives the impression that they are somehow superior to the rest of the group and don't have to follow the rules. If you wait for the chit-chat to subside or make your staff wait while you complete a telephone call you send a message that their time isn't important and their efforts aren't meaningful. Can you imagine how far you would be willing to stretch to help someone who showed so little consideration for your time and efforts?

Step Two - First and foremost find examples of successes, individual and group, that your staff has enjoyed so that you can honestly discuss performance with which you were pleased.

If you decide to use examples involving individuals, try to have something positive to say about everyone, no matter how small the success might have been. Anyone left out will feel slighted or, worse yet, think you aren't happy with their work. You are trying to create an openness and receptivity toward the system. Slighting people will not accomplish that result.

Openly discuss successes and let the employees know you are simply trying to replicate those successes more consistently. If you don't compliment your employees on their successes they will assume the **Making The Exceptional** Normal system is designed to rectify their poor performance. You cannot expect exceptional results if your staff is concerned about job security.

Step Three - Let them know that you have come across a system you believe will allow all of you to become even more successful and valuable to the company while reducing the level of stress in your jobs.

Define the system as a weekly meeting lasting no more than two hours. The purpose of the meeting will be to review everyone's "to do" list and set priorities so that, as a team, you can be assured that the most important tasks are being completed first. State your belief that the only obstacle to greater success is that the "big picture" has not been shared with them. This system is designed to allow them not only to share that vision, but to shape it.

Explain that stress in their jobs will be diminished when the team identifies and eliminates unnecessary tasks or finds more effective ways to accomplish the more mundane work that <u>must</u> be done.

Step Four - Remind each of them that they will experience weeks where the workload is heavy and others where it is lighter. Explain that the success of the team depends on their willingness to pitch in and help someone with a heavier load. Let them know that everyone gains from that experience:

- the helpers add variety, learning and growth to their jobs
- those helped experience less stress in their jobs

- over time, the cross-training that occurs allows each of them to more thoroughly enjoy their vacations by assuring that the workload in the weeks just before and after vacation are easier
- the team's effectiveness increases making all team members more valuable to the company

NOTE: The sequence of these benefits is important. I have listed the items of greatest importance to *them* first. The company's benefit is last. As I have mentioned on several occasions, if you take care of the needs of others they will take care of yours. They will repay your consideration by increasing team effectiveness.

Step Five - Let them know that you will be developing projects which will require their help. Tell them that your projects will face the same scrutiny as theirs when priorities are being set and *mean it.*

Step Six - Ask them whether they have any questions or concerns about the system. Answer all questions honestly. Remember to state the advantages they gain first and the advantages for the company last.

Allay any fears they may have about this being a veiled plan for future staff reductions. Don't raise the issue unless you really sense the unspoken concern. If they express or you sense this concern explain that your goal is to increase the team's ability to accomplish more while the company grows. Remind them that revenue growth combined with increased productivity assures, as much as possible, the job security they seek.

Don't be timid or become defensive when faced with remarks about the lack of job security in the corporate world. Acknowledge it as a fact of life not of your creation. Remind them that one of the reasons you chose this system was to help protect their jobs by increasing their value to the company.

Step Seven - Begin the process by having each person review their work schedule and the priorities they assigned to those tasks. Reach a consensus with that individual about their goals and priorities before moving onto the next person.

Realize that each review will add new information about the "big picture" which may require that earlier goals and priorities be revisited and altered. Make sure that your employees understand that as well.

Keep your own list of the goals and priorities of each employee. This list will form the basis for the subsequent meeting's review.

If you disagree with a person's priorities, don't tell them that you disagree. Rather ask questions that require them to verbalize the benefits of completing each of the tasks where you feel poor priority decisions have been made.

If the person is overlooking an important benefit, find a way to communicate that oversight in question form, "Would you be able to shorten the time on project Y if you did X first?". Once the person realizes that an important factor in the decision has been overlooked he or she will usually fall into line with your view of what the priorities should be.

Don't be afraid to pull rank if necessary, but only as a last resort. In 25 years in management, the number of times I have had to use that ploy can be counted on the fingers of one hand.

If your questions demonstrate that *you* have missed an important aspect in the priority decision (it is inevitable), acknowledge their well thought out conclusion and thank them for helping you see the picture more clearly. You gain respect for being honest enough to admit that you don't have all the answers and that you aren't always right. In the process you credit them with wisdom and encourage their future participation. They will find it easier to change positions when you have demonstrated a willingness to do so.

NOTE: The use of questions to clarify priorities avoids the natural resistance which occurs when people disagree. A question simply asks for more information. A statement that openly disagrees with another's position creates defensiveness. Which do you think would be more successful? How do you respond to each approach?

Make sure that each person is stretching to achieve a little more than they think possible. Tell them that you won't beat up on them if they don't accomplish those extra items, but let them know that you believe they can do it and would like to see them try.

Most people will not disappoint you when they sense that your confidence in them is genuine. If, however, they believe that the statement of confidence is flattery designed to accomplish your goal, they will not participate in the charade.

Step Eight - Once you have completed all the reviews ask them whether they feel that, as a team, they have achieved a worthwhile plan. Don't be surprised if, in the first few meetings, you hear expressions of concern over the aggressiveness of the plan. This is a natural reaction; people don't like to promise more than they can deliver. Don't back down. Rather let them know that you realize this is the initial effort and, as the weeks go by, everyone will be better able to judge what can and can't be done. Then restate your trust in the group's ability to accomplish the plan as drafted.

Step Nine - Set a regular meeting schedule. If they offer reasons why an alternative day or time would be better, listen to them, state your appreciation for their desire to make this effort successful, find a time that resolves most of the time conflicts (it is doubtful that you will be able to satisfy everyone), then set the day and time for your regular meeting.

Let the employees know that at the next meeting each of them will be expected to review their accomplishments from the previous week and establish new goals and priorities for the coming week.

These steps are designed as a checklist to provide consistency in your meetings. It also serves as a reminder of the importance of the use of questions rather than statements to gain buy-in and implementation. Finally, it emphasizes the importance of stating employee benefits before company benefits in creating an atmosphere where the employees are receptive to the changes that this system entails.

NO SYSTEM, regardless of how well designed, will work without the employees trust and belief that their interests are being considered.

11

Subsequent Meetings

All subsequent meetings are designed to:

- review the successes of the previous week
- identify obstacles that prevented success
- establish new goals and priorities for the coming week

You have laid a wonderful foundation for future success, but it is a fragile structure. The foundation is built on trust. Trust takes a lifetime to earn and only a few seconds to lose.

As long as your team *knows* that you have their best interests at heart you will retain their trust. Your occasional mistakes will readily be forgiven as long as your team believes that your intentions are good. Let's discuss how to not only retain but enhance your team's trust in you while dealing with the three components of subsequent meetings.

REVIEW AND PROBLEM IDENTIFICATION
As each team member enumerates the tasks completed, check them against your list from the previous week.

Success - If the person achieved or exceeded the goals set the previous week recognize their accomplishments with *genuine* praise. This shouldn't be too hard because his or her success is your success.

Don't limit your praise to only the "big ticket" items; occasionally note the completion of smaller yet essential tasks. This will assure that your team understands that all tasks regardless of size are important to the team's success.

Disappointment - Remember my earlier caveat that all problems are to be viewed initially as system problems? If someone does not achieve all that they said they would, ask first "What obstacles did you run into that prevented you from achieving your goals?"

The answer will usually fall into one of two categories:

- they allowed themselves to be distracted by other work
- they ran into difficulty doing the work

Distractions - It is inevitable, especially in the first three or four meetings, that someone will revert back to doing what they like rather than doing what they committed to do. Ask them, "Did you see some new benefits from the project that you completed over the one we had agreed was a priority?"

If the answer is yes and you agree with their analysis, applaud their judgment. You want them to be thinking about what they are doing, not just during the planning process, but at all stages of implementation.

What should you do when they feel their reevaluation of the workload warranted a change of plan and you don't agree with their analysis? Obviously, you don't want to discourage course corrections where appropriate, nor do you want them coming to you every time that they feel something has changed.

An approach, which has worked well for me, is the use of questions that allow me to understand their thought processes. Then, using the insights gained, I ask other questions designed to help them see where they overlooked an important aspect of that decision. This approach avoids the negative energy that criticism creates. It also gives the team member a chance to learn how to become more effective in making future decisions.

It is unlikely that someone will simply refuse to do the planned work, but anything is possible and we need to be able to deal with any eventuality. The tool of choice in dealing with this situation is, once again, the question. The purpose of our questions is to gain insights into why this team member didn't *honor their commitment to the team*. This phrase is powerful because it shifts the attention from what you expected to what the team expected thereby removing personal conflict from the discussion.

If the answers to your exploratory questions aren't satisfactory remain silent about your feelings. Simply ask them whether the team can count on them to honor their future commitments. Peer pressure will work its magic in gaining their agreement and future performance.

Silence may seem like an unlikely response, but if we review our discussion of trust in Chapter 7, we will remember that people trust that we will not criticize them in front of their peers nor will we talk about their inadequacies with others. The absence of praise does not violate these conditions for trust.

When you have consistently praised others for their success and withhold comment when disappointed, your message of displeasure is sent as loudly and more effectively than if you had been openly critical. The other team members will appreciate your wisdom in not ruining the positive tenor of the meeting by becoming openly confrontational. You will be viewed favorably by the rest of the team while the offending team member senses that their status has diminished.

Your response to this difficult situation will gain you the respect of your team and, possibly, the offending member as well. Your actions will demonstrate your commitment to earning their trust everyday and they will feel that their trust in you is well placed.

What do you do next? Give the person another chance. You have sent your message. Allow the person time to consider the error of their ways and to rectify them for the next meeting. Don't have a special pow-wow with them to discuss their inadequacies; there is always time for that approach. If they sign on to make the system work in future meetings you will have gained the outcome you desired while avoiding an uncomfortable and unnecessary confrontation. You will also gain their respect for not having overreacted to their mistake. In chapter 13 we will discuss how to deal with those who won't accept their responsibility to the team.

Another type of distraction occurs when a team member tries to squeeze in a small project only to find that it is more time consuming than originally anticipated. It is human nature to want to complete what we have started so the person continues the project to its completion at the expense of a higher priority effort.

Applaud their intentions. They were trying to increase the team's success. Tell them that you understand and appreciate what they were trying to do. Let them know that, in the future, you want them to leave the lesser important projects go until all priority items are complete. You are not scolding them, rather you are reinforcing the importance of the plan. Don't hesitate to make that statement for the benefit of all team members.

Difficulty with the work - This is good news! Whenever a person has problems accomplishing a task you have identified an opportunity for improvement. These situations allow the group to explore the methods employed in performing the task. Each member of the team will bring his or her intelligence, creativity and experience to bear on the question, "Is there a better way?"

"I have never seen perfection, so I *know* there must be a better way" is a motto that has served me well over the years. This attitude helps me:

- to continuously reevaluate what is being done
- keep my mind open to all ideas offered
- avoid the comfort trap, "it has worked well in the past"

I hope you will adopt this attitude and employ it in team meetings so that others can experience its power as well.

Each time your team diminishes the complexity of a task, eliminates unnecessary work or removes wasted effort from your collective workloads they:

- gain the satisfaction of knowing their work has value
- reduce stress
- believe they can accomplish even more

These benefits sustain their efforts for continuous improvement while making your job easier and more fun.

Don't bemoan difficulties, rather recognize them for what they are - *opportunities for a better tomorrow.*

ESTABLISH NEW GOALS AND PRIORITIES
You need only follow steps four through nine of the meeting checklist in Chapter 8 to create your plan for the coming week.

NEW ROLES
Your meeting roles are teacher, coach and cheering section.

You teach them to become more effective when you ask questions that help them develop their decision-making abilities. You coach them by leading them through the process of goal setting, priority setting and focused implementation. You become their cheering section when you praise their accomplishments and take no credit for yourself.

They will quickly come to understand and appreciate what you contribute to their success. The recognition will come more quickly if you don't appear to be concerned about it.

Finally, use some simple reward systems to celebrate their success. Have pizza or ice cream brought in for the meeting. Occasionally send them home a half hour or hour early. Be sure that the time off relates directly to some exceptional performance and state your belief that they earned it.

These simple acts demonstrate both your appreciation for the team's efforts and your joy in their success.

12

Opposite Ends of the Spectrum

Most of the people on your team will respond very well to the system and approaches outlined thus far. They will follow your lead and experience the joys of variety, learning, growth and success on the job.

There are two categories of people who will pose particular challenges to your management skills, the overly optimistic and the excessively cautious. As you can see they are on opposite ends of the spectrum.

The Overly Optimistic
Overly optimistic people assume that they will always be successful. They seldom consider whether they have the necessary skills and experience to do the job. If they do, they aren't usually honest with themselves about whether

they possess the tools necessary to do the job. Nor are they realistic about the time needed to do a good job.

The overly optimistic are easy to spot. They consistently establish impossible goals for themselves. You know it. Their teammates know it. Everyone knows it but the person setting the goals. The overly optimistic will be the first to volunteer to help a teammate after having just set impossible goals for themselves.

The question is "How do we let them know that they are overreaching without dampening their enthusiasm?" An approach that has worked well for me involves the following steps:

- thank them for setting such aggressive goals
- let them know that you feel that they have set a challenging week for themselves
- tell them which tasks you would like them to focus on and which goals you expect them to accomplish in the coming week
- state that you consider anything more "icing on the cake"
- let them know you won't be disappointed if they don't achieve everything they set out to do

This approach avoids statements which might create the impression that you mistrust their abilities, integrity, realism or self-image.

The Excessively Cautious
On the other end of the spectrum we have people who for whatever reason are concerned about promising more than they can deliver. So much so that they are unwilling

to commit to what we consider a "slam dunk, no brainer, do it in your sleep" set of goals.

What we want to do with this group is ask them to set what *they* consider stretch goals. They will resist, but tell them, repeatedly if necessary, that you believe that they can do it. Let them know that you don't think they are giving themselves enough credit for their skills and abilities.

The key to the success of this approach is that *you* must be certain they can accomplish what you ask. If you set them up for failure, whatever is causing their caution will be intensified and their resistance to future stretch goals will be greater.

By assuring their success week in and week out over a period of months you enable them to see their real potential. They will gradually become more aggressive in setting their own goals. Each new success intensifies their belief that they can accomplish whatever they wish. One of your greatest joys as a manager will be seeing someone in this category blossom into a self-assured, happy, successful employee.

13

Dealing with Poor Performers

Despite your best efforts there will always be some
people who simply won't get with the program. There
was a young man on my staff at the mortgage banking
firm who repeatedly failed to honor his commitments.

During our first private meeting, I assumed the blame for
not having communicated well what was expected of him
or the importance of the work. I restated the goals and
asked him whether he had any questions. He had none.

A month later, I wasn't seeing any improvement so we
had another private meeting. I asked him why we weren't
seeing better results. He had no explanation. I asked
whether he understood what was expected of him. He
said that he did. I asked him to state the goals we had

agreed to and explain why they were important. He did. I told him that if he didn't begin performing according to expectation, the next meeting would result in his dismissal. He said he understood.

Two weeks later I had to fire this young man. On his way out the door he turned to me and said, "I hope you find someone who will accomplish what you want." To this day I have no idea why he chose to forego his job.

Anyone who manages eventually has to fire. While the **Making The Exceptional** Normal system doesn't eliminate this unpleasant task, it will dramatically reduce the number of times you have to engage in this activity. Your team's enjoyment of their work combined with the exceptional results they produce will make the need to fire a rarity.

You will be pleased to learn of another system benefit as it relates to the firing situation. One of the advantages of the group meeting is that everyone gets to see who is performing and who is not.

Over time the performers begin to resent the underperformers. When you fire the underperformers you will be surprised to find that you don't experience the usual morale problems associated with a firing. Quite the contrary, the performers feel that their actions are affirmed.

The performers know that they are doing what they are supposed to do. They also know that the underperformers aren't. The performers will have watched you give the underperformers numerous opportunities to improve their performance. You will have demonstrated a willingness to go the extra mile to help the underperformers. They will have seen the underperformers mock your efforts by wasting every opportunity.

The performers, knowing that you have put forth more effort than the underperformers, will understand the futility of your efforts and support your decision to fire.

14

Vision

As you employ the *Making The Exceptional* Normal system you will experience a change in your work that will be simultaneously gratifying and disconcerting. You will have more free time.

You no longer have to "follow up" to assure that things are going to be done on time. Your employees will come to you with fewer questions because they know what they need to do. The time once lost to these activities is now available to you.

This reality, coupled with the fact that your employees have come to *expect* variety, new challenges, learning opportunities and growth in their jobs, place upon you a need to develop new initiatives for your team to tackle. This can be a frightening prospect. It requires you to have a vision of the future and many of you don't view yourselves as visionaries.

Take heart, vision is not a genetically-acquired trait. Doubt that? Try this little experiment. The next time you are involved in a conversation with a person who has a strong interest in whatever topic you are discussing, ask them:

- how will things be different in the future?
- what changes do you anticipate?
- what will drive those changes ?

Their responses represent their vision for the future for that topic.

Repeat the experiment with people from all walks of life, with varying levels of education and socioeconomic standing and you will find that in the areas that interest them most, they have vision of what the future will bring. Notice that I did not say the vision was correct, I merely said they have vision. Let's gain a little more understanding of what's involved in creating a vision before we discuss how to increase its accuracy.

Creating a vision
Vision is created when we combine knowledge, interest, awareness and deductive reasoning.

Knowledge forms the basis for our vision. If we don't have a thorough understanding of how something works today, how can we hope to predict how it will work in the future. Who could possibly have envisioned satellite communications without first understanding how sound travels? If we use a missile launch analogy, knowledge is the launch pad for our vision.

Interest is the fuel that drives our exploration of alternatives. Unless we have an interest in the subject we will not invest the time or energy looking for improvements to the status quo.

Awareness serves as our monitor to make sure that our trajectory is true. Awareness and interest are closely aligned. The stronger our interest the more aware we are of new information that can impact the future. Information acquired by virtue of our awareness expands our knowledge base for future launches.

Deductive reasoning allows us to make course corrections when awareness provides new information. It is through this process that we take what we know and what we are learning and combine them into a vision of what the future can be. More importantly, if we don't like what the future holds, deductive reasoning will help us find ways to impact the way the future is evolving.

By combining knowledge, interest, awareness and deductive reasoning you can become a visionary for your organization.

Clarity
A common misconception about vision is that it is always clear. We don't awaken with clear vision, so how is it that we expect our first glimpse of the future to have clarity? Unless all the components described above are in place, the vision may never become clear. Let me give you a personal example.

In 1982 I was talking to a friend who was one of the founders and a member of the board of directors of a successful hospital. They were building a new MRI unit.

When I asked him why they didn't partner with some of the other hospitals in the area to build a centrally-located facility, his response was that they had to have their own unit to be competitive.

By now I am sure you realize that I have a financial background. His response tapped into my knowledge of finance and economics which says that when businesses add capacity that exceeds demand, severe financial ramifications are inevitable. As a purchaser of health insurance and a potential consumer of hospital services, I had an interest in the future of health care costs.

Awareness, created by news reports about an excess supply of hospital beds, told me that the hospitals were very likely creating a financial crisis. Reason told me that something would have to change in the future.

While I had a vision that significant changes in health care were on the horizon, I could not predict the timing, direction or magnitude of the changes. I lacked adequate knowledge of how hospitals, insurance companies and Medicare interact to develop a clear picture of what the future of health care might be. Could I have clarified that vision? Absolutely, but it would have required more resources than I had available to study these three aspects of the health care industry.

The accuracy of your vision is enhanced as interest and awareness produce new information for deductive reasoning to consider. Sometimes that occurs naturally without any conscious effort on your part. At other times the result comes from your concerted effort to learn more about what the future holds and how you might impact that future. The active, conscious approach affords you greater influence in shaping the future.

As a manager you are responsible for:

- visualizing the opportunities for future growth
- evaluating the value of various growth opportunities
- working to clarify the vision
- converting the vision to goals
- blending these goals into your team's efforts

Use the free time that the **Making The Exceptional** Normal system affords you to talk with others in your organization. Get a glimpse of their visions. Think about how their vision impacts yours. Repeat this process at regular intervals, at least monthly, and you will assure that the wells of variety, challenge, learning and growth never go dry for your employees.

15

A Manager's Dream

In the blissful peace of slumber a manager dreams of:

- a romantic weekend
- attending the kids' sporting events
- reading a book for entertainment
- planning a family excursion
- spending time with parents, friends and loved ones

Enjoy the dreams. Your success at Making The Exceptional Normal will allow them to become reality. You will no longer engage in activities that sap your strength; things like:

- following up to make sure the work is done
- bemoaning the fact that work didn't get done in the sequence you desired
- scrambling to avoid missing deadlines
- watching work pile up because you and your team are moving from one crisis to another

All of these activities have, at one time or another, exacted tolls in your energy level, your feeling that you could make a difference, your desire to try and even your mental and physical health. They have robbed you of time with loved ones, deprived you of memories and left you wondering where you lost control. This doesn't have to be your future.

The exceptional results that you and your team produce will energize you. More will be accomplished with less effort, leaving plenty of time and energy for things other than work. You will truly have time to recreate yourselves.

You and your team are too valuable. Don't let your collective skills, abilities, creativity and passion for life be wasted when *you* have the capacity for **Making The Exceptional** Normal.

A Final Thought

Throughout this book I have tried to help you experience the emotions associated with the various stages of the **Making The Exceptional** Normal system. My purpose was twofold.

I didn't want you to have to take my word about why this system works. I wanted you to be able to validate the concepts with your emotions and life experiences. The more intuitive your understanding the greater the likelihood you will employ the system effectively and reap its benefits.

The second reason for this approach is to let you know that the answers to situations not covered in this book reside within you. I cannot envision all the situations you might face much less cover them in a single book. Fortunately, that isn't necessary.

When faced with an unusual situation all you need to do is follow these simple steps:

- suspend thoughts about what you want
- think about why your needs or desires might not coincide with those of your employees; did you consider WIIFT (what's in it for them) before seeking their involvement?
- spend time talking with the individual to find the source of their reluctance to provide what you want
- maintain a non-judgmental, solution-oriented approach so that the employee knows that you don't consider their actions a personal affront or an indication that they are incompetent
- use the information gained to find a way for both of you to get as much of what you want as possible (don't load the scales in your favor)

Even though each of us is unique, there is a commonality to our humanity that allows us to anticipate the needs and desires of others. When you tap into your understanding of these needs you enable yourself to anticipate the other person's needs and make provision for them in your plans. Taking care of the needs of others is the most effective way to assure that your needs are met. This approach works as well in your personal life as in business.

It is my sincere wish that by sharing the insights gained from 25 years in various management roles I can make your work life easier, enjoyable and more fulfilling.

Dale Furtwengler

Making The EXCEPTIONAL NORMAL
BENEFITS OF THE WEEKLY MEETING

A weekly meeting requiring less than 2 hours will allow you to:

- make planning fun
- assure that all team members have goals for the coming week
- establish priorities for those goals
- create a shared vision
- give employees a sense for how they fit into the "big picture"
- identify system inefficiencies (needless work and time-consuming approaches)
- give employees the satisfaction of determining their own plans
- establish accountability for results
- create an opportunity for them to experience more enjoyment in their jobs than they have experienced in quite some time

Making The EXCEPTIONAL NORMAL
MEETING CHECKLIST

☐ Start on time.

☐ Find examples of successes to discuss so that they are assured that this is an improvement effort not displeasure with past performance.

☐ Discuss the inevitability of workload disparity and that you will be looking to them to ensure that the most important group goals are achieved first. The benefits to them are variety, learning opportunities and personal growth

☐ Assure them that there will be no paucity of work. Let them know that you have a list of projects awaiting their attention.

☐ Have each person list their goals and priorities for the coming week. Reach consensus with the individual before moving onto the next person.

☐ Ask for their opinion of the plan. Are they satisfied with the goals and priorities for the coming week. Has anything been overlooked?

Making The EXCEPTIONAL NORMAL
KEYS TO BUY-IN & IMPLEMENTATION

DO:

- Make sure that every employee knows that you view inefficiencies as system problems and not performance problems
- Ask them to estimate the time required for each task on their list
- When a task appears to take longer to perform than seems reasonable ask, "What is it that requires so much time?" (this verbiage reinforces your earlier statement that you view all problems as system problems)
- Solicit the help of others in the group to find less time-consuming approaches to completing the task
- State your belief that they have the intelligence and creativity to find a better way to perform the task
- Pay close attention to employees' concerns
- Gain consensus time-saving approaches
- Implement quickly
- **Recognize the contributors for their insights**

Making The EXCEPTIONAL NORMAL
KEYS TO BUY-IN & IMPLEMENTATION

DON'T:

- Use language that assigns blame
- Question the ability of an employee in the presence of others
- Question an employee's motives in front of others
- Verbalize doubts about an employee's ability to do the job
- Ignore the employee's concerns about an alternative solution
- Create opportunities for failure

INDEX

Q

Questions
..attitude toward, 57
..sample, 17-21

R

Respect, 29, 72

S

Shared vision, 26
Sharing the burden, 23
Silence, 83
Solutions, 103
Subsequent meetings
..disappointment,80
..manager's roles, 84
..problem identification, 80
..review, 79
..setting new goals, 84
..success, 80
System – key elements, 11

T

Team spirit, 30
Trust
..how to gain, 52
..overview, 12
..what must they trust?, 55

U

Underestimating employee
skills, 45

V

Variety, 41
Vision
..awareness, 97
..deductive reasoning, 97
..interest, 97
..knowledge, 96
..manager's reponsibility, 99
..shared, 26

W

WIIFT, 72
Workforce flexibility, 29
Workload allocation, 28, 74
Work preferences, 18
..interest, 19
..skills, 20

ABOUT THE AUTHOR

Dale Furtwengler is a consultant, speaker and author. He is the President of Furtwengler & Associates, P.C, a firm dedicated to helping managers link financial success and operational performance. Dale is the author of three seminars, *Question Your Way To Success, Making The Exceptional Normal and Taking Charge of Your Company's Finances.*

NOTES

NOTES

NOTES

NOTES